Baggage Claim

A Modern Day Parable

By Don Bosley

Copyright © 2006 by Don Bosley. All print rights administered by Lillenas Publishing Co. All rights reserved. Printed in the United States.

All scripture quotations are from the *Holy Bible, New International Version*® (NIV®). Copyright © 1973, 1978, 1984 by International Bible Society. Used by permission of Zondervan Publishing House. All rights reserved.

 The purchase of this play entitles the purchaser to make photocopies of the material for use in their church or nonprofit organization. The sharing of this material with other churches or organizations not owned or controlled by the original purchaser is strictly prohibited. The contents of this play may not be reproduced in any other form without written permission from the publisher.
 This play is protected by copyright laws. No edits or changes may be made to the script without advanced permission from the author. Please contact Lillenas Drama for more information on copyright laws.
 This is a royalty play. Permission for amateur performance of this work is granted when a script is purchased by your organization, and the royalty is paid two weeks prior to the performance(s). The performance licensing fee for this play is $35.00 for the first performance and $25.00 for each subsequent performance. Please use the form found on the following page to register your performance(s) and to submit the royalty payment.

The following should appear in your printed program:
 "Produced by special arrangement with Lillenas Publishing Co."

Questions? Please write, call, or E-mail:
 Lillenas® Publishing Company
 Drama Resources
 P.O. Box 419527
 Kansas City, MO 64141
 Phone: 816-931-1900 • Fax: 816-412-8390
 E-mail: drama@lillenas.com
 Web Site: www.lillenasdrama.com

"In my Father's house
are many rooms . . .
I am going there to
prepare a place for you."
(John 14:2)

Dedication

To the One who came to me on the precipice,
and bid me to take a leap . . .

Contents

Production Notes	7
Synopsis	7
Cast	7
Props	8
Costumes	8
Setting	8
Act II Opener Notes	9
Other Production Notes	9
Baggage Claim	11
Appendix	61
Music Notes	61
Performance License	63

Production Notes

SYNOPSIS

Baggage Claim is a drama that was written and designed for outreach. It is a parable that, at its core, lays out the gospel of Jesus Christ in imagery that can be grasped by a contemporary audience—attempting to follow the model that Jesus himself gave in the telling of His own parables.

The story is built around a modern-day family on vacation at a much-publicized Bed & Breakfast, located on the mile-high precipice of a deep canyon. Their New Year's Eve stay goes awry, however, when they find that the lodge is full of animated goofballs, while a screwy bellhop keeps tossing their entire luggage into the cavernous canyon. Sam, the father, becomes increasingly unraveled as he has to keep traversing 347 flights of stairs to retrieve his stuff.

Comedic beginnings segue into a darker reality as we begin to see the pain and inner conflicts of the four family members. But one by one they begin to willingly turn over their baggage to the bellhop, gradually recognizing that he is in fact Jesus Christ. Sam keeps resisting—until, just one stroke before midnight, he is stunned to realize that the bill is too big for him to pay. When the bellhop sacrifices his own life to pay it, Sam finally understands.

CAST:

SAM D'BAQUEL—A gravy salesman
IRENE—Sam's wife
EDDIE—Their 20 year-old son
BRITTANY—Their 17 year-old daughter
JAKE—Hotel Bellhop/Handyman
CLARISSE—Hotel Desk Clerk
LEONARD—Guest
OMA—Guest
SABRINA—Guest
FRANKLIN—Guest
Other assorted guests

PROPS:

Laptop computer
Cell phone
About 15-20 pieces of luggage, various sizes
One large sales trunk
A hotel luggage cart
Bed & Breakfast Brochure
Hotel desk bell
Tablecloth
Glasses of punch
Kitchen knife
Baseball bat and duffel bag
Vodka bottle
Sam's "burdens"
Party blowers, hats, favors
Glow-in-the-dark rope for tying up Brittany
Bible

COSTUMES:

SAM—Business suit and tie
IRENE—June Cleaver-type mom dress
BRITTANY—Cheerleader outfit, or, better yet—warm-ups
EDDIE—Contemporary young guy's look, i.e, wrinkled overshirt, loose pocket shorts, headphones
JAKE—Nothing special, servant-suitable
CLARISSE—Casual business attire
GUESTS—Anything goes
DEMONS—Black from head to toe, including hoods; white masks or face paint can be effective

SETTING

Lobby of the Crossroads Bed & Breakfast—present day. It is pretty simple as B&Bs go, with worn old sofas and chairs, a bookcase or two, a check-in counter, and a large breakfast table. Upstage is a large double-door entrance from outdoors; when the door is open, a sturdy porch railing is all that separates visitors from a vast canyon below. There is also a telescope at the window for looking out over the canyon. Elsewhere upstage is an entrance from a hallway.

Download a drawing of the set at www.lillenas.com

ACT II OPENER NOTES

The opening scene of Act II is deliberately designed to slam the story into a different dimension. From the frivolity that characterized the end of Act I, we're suddenly faced with our perky cheerleader holding a knife to her wrist—and all the dark isolation that this implies for Brittany and other characters. To depict the raging conflict within, we utilized some dark, desperate music and some pretty menacing, relentless demons. Everywhere Brittany tries to run, the demons cut her off. We used intermittent strobes and a glow-in-the-dark rope to depict the demons tying her up with her own sin. When Jake (Jesus) comes on the scene and scatters the demons, he then picks up the knife from the ground and cuts her free.

The whole experience is like a dream in the back of Brittany's mind, and at this point she is even unaware of the one who has delivered her and stayed her suicidal hand. When the scene ends and the innocent party music comes up again, she drops right back into that reality, albeit a little dazed. She will recognize her deliverer, and the magnitude of his restorative hand, later.

Essentially, even if your demons are not "dancers" per se, the scene can still play like a powerful human video. Selection of the right music is paramount here.

OTHER PRODUCTION NOTES

- If you're going to include dance or human video elements in your show, it's helpful to cast many of the B&B guests as these performers.
- Jake's deliberate fall into the canyon is a potentially dramatic moment in the show. One technique to emphasize it is to put "scrim curtains" over the balcony doors and backlight it. When Jake moves to the balcony, closes the door behind him and stands on the edge, his striking silhouette is then transmitted to the audience. He can even take a crucifix position before falling into the canyon.
- From our set designer, John Klonowski: Baggage Claim is a difficult show to do abstractly, because there are certain physical requirements that the script calls for in regards to the set (Example: the balcony/window where Jake throws the suit-

cases over and the comedic moments after they come trudging up the stairs). The set design should also be sensitive to the climactic moment, when Jake jumps off the balcony. This should be highly visible to most, if not all, of the audience.

Act I

SCENE 1

(Lights up. The B&B lobby is empty. The front door bangs open. A weary hand plops a large, heavy suitcase through the door. SAM, *breathing heavily, half-falls into the room.)*

JAKE *(arriving)*: Good afternoon, sir.

*(*SAM *nods at him wearily, then reaches back out the door for the rest of his luggage. All manner of suitcases, shoulder bags, and other luggage are tying him up this time.* JAKE *feints and moves with him, trying to figure out how to help. After a titanic struggle,* SAM *essentially spills into the room, in a heap amongst his luggage.* JAKE *tries to help him, but* SAM'S *frustrated flailing is only making the entanglement worse. Finally* SAM *struggles to his knees, leaning on one large suitcase.)*

JAKE: Welcome to the Crossroads Bed & Breakfast.

*(*SAM *tries to speak, but all he does is wheeze. He tries again; same result.* JAKE *reaches into a nearby bowl full of ice, pulls out a bottled water and hands it to him.* SAM *nods his gratitude . . . but when he tries to twist off the top of the bottle, it won't twist. He tries a little harder. Then he goes at it almost frantically, and when that fails, he is almost whimpering. He begins banging it against the suitcase. Presently* JAKE *takes the bottle gently and twists off the top for him.* SAM *gulps down the water desperately, spilling it all over his suit. Still gasping,* SAM *thumbs over his shoulder wearily.)*

SAM: Three— *(gasp, gasp)* Three— *(gasp, gasp)* Three— *(gasp)*

JAKE *(guessing)*: Three . . . syllables. First syllable . . .

*(*SAM *shakes his head no.)*

JAKE *(watching* SAM*)*: Uh, negative. Nein. Nyet. Sounds like nyet.

*(*SAM *holds up a hand to erase and make him stop.)*

JAKE *(guessing)*: Wave. Hello. Goodbye. Wax on, wax off.

(SAM *slumps in resignation. He gathers himself to speak.*)

SAM *(indicating the canyon):* Three . . . hundred . . . *(gasp)* . . . and forty-seven . . . *(gasp)* . . . flights of stairs . . .

JAKE: That's more than three syllables.

(SAM *stares at him.*)

JAKE: Oh! *(Getting it)* Oh, 347 flights of stairs! You just came up our 347 flights of stairs!

(SAM *nods wearily.*)

JAKE: Invigorating, isn't it?

(SAM *looks at him like he's nuts.*)

JAKE: My name is Jake, sir. May I help you with your bags?

SAM: Now he asks. No, thank you, I think I can manage from here.

(SAM *moves unsteadily to balcony. He peers over the railing stage left to the canyon below.*)

SAM *(yelling down):* Just stay close to the canyon wall, kids! And don't look down—not even to admire the clouds!

JAKE *(as* SAM *reenters):* Do you have a reservation, sir?

SAM *(sarcastic):* No, I just thought I'd climb Mount Everest out there to come and get a brochure. *(Dusting himself off)* You run this place, Jake?

JAKE: Actually, I'm more of a part-handyman, part-bellhop, part-gardener.

SAM: Yeah? You'd think one of your parts would learn how to install a stinkin' elevator!

JAKE *(smile):* Good one, sir.

SAM: I don't know what you people are thinking. This isn't a bed-and-breakfast. This is what Army Rangers do for truth-or-dare.

(*Suddenly there is a shriek from offstage, startling* SAM. LEONARD *sprints into the lobby, shrieking with great excitement and exaggerated animation. He shrieks and jumps in place, shrieks at the audience, even grabs* SAM *by the lapels and shrieks at him. Eventually* LEONARD *sprints right back in the direction he came, shrieking all the way.* SAM *is deadpan-expression through all of this, watching blankly as* LEONARD *departs. He looks at* JAKE *for an explanation.* JAKE *only smiles back.*)

SAM: That person just get their bill?

(IRENE *peers in the doorway and excitedly claps her hands together.*)

IRENE: Oh, wow! Wow, wow, wow!

SAM: Yeah, you can say that again, Irene. Wow.

(SAM *begins to check his cell phone messages.*)

IRENE: Oh, it's amazing! (*Squeezing into the room with her own luggage*) Just amazing! (*To* JAKE.) Hi, I'm Irene.

JAKE (*shaking her hand warmly*): Jake. Pleasure to have you. Help you with your bags?

IRENE (*waving him off*): Oh, I'm fine! Oh, this place is utterly fantastic! I mean, Sam, admit it: it's utterly fantastic!

SAM (*flatly*): It's utterly fantastic, Irene.

IRENE: Isn't it? Fantastic!

SAM: Fantastic.

IRENE: Utterly!

SAM: The utterliest.

IRENE (*at the telescope*): Oh, and this view! Incredible, Jake! Just incredible! You can see for miles from here!

SAM: You can see a cardiologist from here.

IRENE: The world-famous Crossroads Bed & Breakfast! What a perfect, perfect place for our family to spend New Year's Eve! Oh, Sam, it's just like I imagined it.

SAM *(checking palm pilot):* Oh, yeah, me too. I've often said, "Boy, take me away from the glamour and the parties and the fun, and give me a New Year's Eve on a cliff overlooking a dry and dusty desert canyon! That's where the real action is!"

IRENE *(excitedly, to* JAKE*):* Oh, now, do tell: Is "the man" himself here this weekend?

JAKE: I'm sorry?

IRENE: Innkeeper Fred! The legendary proprietor of your legendary establishment!

JAKE: Oh, yes. Of course. Innkeeper Fred is always here.

IRENE: Do you hear that, Sam? He's here!

SAM: Great. Why don't you ask if he was the one that just ran through the lobby screaming like his boxers are on fire.

IRENE: What are you talking about, Sam?

SAM: I'm talking about some crazy shrieker, Irene! Just now.

EDDIE *(poking head in front door):* Dude! No way! Where's a streaker?

*(*SAM *glares at* EDDIE*.)*

SAM: I didn't say "streaker," I said "shrieker." Shrieker. All right? As in, a shrieking person.

EDDIE: Oh. *(Nodding)* Right on . . .

SAM *(pulling headphones off of one of* EDDIE'S *ears):* You know, son, you might be able to understand people better if you didn't have your music *turned up louder than a nuclear testing range*! For crying out loud, Eddie. If a 747 were landing on your head, do you think you'd even notice?

EDDIE *(shrug):* Probably. I mean, there'd be tire marks, right?

IRENE: Eddie . . . Eddie dear . . . don't you just love this place?

EDDIE: Oh, yeah, Mom. It looks great.

IRENE: And Eddie . . . guess what? *(Barely able to contain)* He's here!

EDDIE: Who is?

SAM: Innkeeper Bob.

IRENE: Fred.

SAM: Bob, Fred, Charlie, who gives a rip? Whoever he is, he needs a new decorator. Look at this place. Gaudy furniture. Bad carpet. I've stayed at a lot of business hotels in my day, but this one ranks right up there with the cheesiest.

IRENE *(with brochure):* Oh, look, look. It says here that, over the years, Innkeeper Fred has served more people than the largest retailers in the world! *(To* JAKE.*)* Is that true?

JAKE: Absolutely true, ma'am.

IRENE: Did you hear that, Sam? Served more people than the largest retailers in the world! Unbelievable!

SAM: I'll say it is.

JAKE *(to* EDDIE*):* May I help you with your bags, sir?

EDDIE *(beginning to hand them over):* Right on . . .

SAM *(to* EDDIE*):* You'll carry your own bags, mister. *(To* IRENE.*)* Always looking for the easy way out, that one. Nothing wrong with a little raw, good old-fashioned sweat, Eddie my boy! Always remember that.

*(*EDDIE *shrugs apologetically at* JAKE.*)*

EDDIE: The Dad.

JAKE: I understand.

*(*BRITTANY *appears in doorway, wearing a cheerleader's outfit and out of breath.)*

BRITTANY *(too happy):* Wooooooo! All right! OK! *(Enters with her bags)* Wow! Three-hundred forty-seven flights! That'll get the ol' pumper going, eh, Dad?

SAM: Brittany, honey, Daddy is so sorry. I didn't know, honestly. Are you OK? *(Fanning her with his hand)* Did you overexert yourself, princess? I hope you didn't overexert yourself!

BRITTANY: Daddy, I'm fine.

SAM *(looking at her forehead):* Good heavens, what is that?

BRITTANY *(alarmed):* Where?

SAM: On your forehead!

BRITTANY: What? Is it a zit? *(Pulling out her compact hurriedly)* Oh, it can't be a zit! It just can't be!

SAM: Well . . .

BRITTANY: I knew it! Ashley McKenzie had a zit in the middle of her forehead last week, and I could tell just by looking at it that it was contagious, but *nooooo*, she swore it wasn't, which is just the kind of thing she always says . . . ugh!

IRENE: Now, calm down, honey.

BRITTANY: She thinks she's all that because her older brother plays football for Notre Dame or Notre Republic or whatever. Like anybody cares! It doesn't change the fact that she's still got a zit in the middle of her forehead, does it!

IRENE: Actually, honey, now it's not a zit at all. See? *(Dabbing at her forehead with a finger)* Just a little perspiration.

BRITTANY: Really? *(Relieved, happy again)* Oh, OK, then. Whew!

SAM *(flipping out):* Perspiration? You mean, she's sweating?

EDDIE *(sounding like his dad):* Nothing wrong with a little raw, good old-fashioned sweat, Brittany, my girl. Always remember that!

SAM: Was anybody asking you? Huh? Get your sister's bags, for crying out loud! Can't you see she's having heatstroke?

JAKE: I'll be happy to assist with her bags . . .

SAM: A lot of good that does her now, now that she's half-dead from your stairs! Never mind—he's got them.

(*Defeated,* EDDIE *sets about taking* BRITTANY's *luggage and stacking it neatly.*)

SAM (*to* BRITTANY): Now, sweetie, we'll all understand if you feel like you've been traumatized. We don't have to stay here if you don't want to.

IRENE: Sam! We are too staying here! You promised we could have this one family getaway.

SAM: Not if it's going to scar our children for life, Irene. Now, Brittany, it's really up to you. Are you OK staying at this place for New Year's? Or would you rather go someplace . . . nice?

BRITTANY: I'm fine, Daddy. Really. My only question is . . . well, are there any boys?

SAM: What?

BRITTANY: Boys, Dad. You know, boys? Like I told you guys when you tried to send me to that private school last year: I don't go places where there are no boys.

SAM: Boys . . . boys. (*Retreating to* IRENE.) See, Irene, we gotta go. There are no boys.

IRENE: I'm sure there are some boys around here somewhere, Sam.

SAM (*returning to* BRITTANY, *uncertainly*): Uh, your mother is sure there are some boys around somewhere, honey.

BRITTANY (*smiling*): Well, I hope not! Boys are all pigs who deserve to be dipped in tar and cast adrift in rotting pond scum!

(SAM *stands flummoxed. He moves slowly to* IRENE, *not taking his eyes off* BRITTANY.)

SAM: Little help?

IRENE: It's the Inverted Bi-Polar Maiden Complex, Sam.

SAM: The what?

IRENE: Inverted Bi-Polar Maiden Complex.

SAM: What in the world does that mean?

EDDIE: It means she's moody.

SAM: You butt out!

IRENE: Her school counselor says it's very common in girls her age.

SAM: My princess has Inverted . . . Bi-Molar . . . Something Whatsits . . . and nobody told me? What do we do?

IRENE: Just roll with it, Sam. Just tell her not to worry—maybe there will be no boys here after all.

SAM *(uncertainly):* Honey, maybe there will be no boys here after all.

BRITTANY *(eye roll):* Daaad, helloooo . . . ! I just told you, I don't go places with no boys!

IRENE: Honestly, Sam, you do need to try and listen to her more.

(SAM *stands speechless, trying to figure out how he lost out here.*)

JAKE: Well, I'm off to do some work in the garden, sir. Make yourself at home, and when you're ready to check in, just ring the bell and the clerk will come and take care of you. Have a wonderful stay.

IRENE *(waving):* Thank you, Jake!

(JAKE *exits to hall.*)

IRENE: What a nice man!

SAM: How do you like that? We have to ring the bell to get somebody to check us in! If this place had any class, there'd be somebody waiting here to check us in, eager to have our business.

IRENE: Jake seemed eager . . .

SAM: Yeah, well, you wouldn't get away with this kind of customer service in the gravy industry, I can tell you that. I forget about John Q. Public for just one second, and boom! — You know what happens?

EDDIE: You're yesterday's gravy?

SAM: Yesterday's gravy! That's exactly right. And I tell you, son, there's no worse fate for a good gravy man. Always remember that.

IRENE: Oh, Sam. Just ring the bell, silly!

SAM: No, I will not ring the bell! Don't you see, Irene? That's just what they want us to do! Why should I have to ring a bell? When people come into our gravy showroom, do they ever have to ring a bell?

EDDIE: Well . . . we don't have a bell in our showroom, Dad.

SAM: Precisely my point! You put out a bell, you're basically telling the customer, "We value you and your potential patronization so very little that instead of standing ready, diligently prepared to serve you with our 31 astonishing gravy flavors, we will require you instead to stretch out your palm and depress an annoying ringing device in order to get our stinking attention!"

EDDIE: I . . . I never thought of it that way.

SAM: Of course you didn't.

BRITTANY: That's why he's the king of the gravy world! *(Head sweetly on* SAM'S *shoulder)*

SAM: Thank you, princess.

IRENE: Well, I'll ring the bell. Maybe Innkeeper Fred himself will answer! *(To* BRITTANY.*)* He's here, you know.

BRITTANY: No! Way?

IRENE: Way!

(IRENE *moves to the counter.)*

BRITTANY *(smiling, to* SAM*)*: Who's Innkeeper Fred?

SAM: No clue.

BRITTANY: OK, then!

(IRENE *rings the bell.* CLARISSE *enters, dancing into the room to an upbeat instrumental, with great animation and flourish. She spends several moments twirling happily and stylishly around the room.* SAM *is unimpressed, and even checks his watch at one point as her dance goes on and on. His family, however, is more captured by* CLARISSE. *When* CLARISSE *finally stops before them, the music abruptly stops with her.*)

CLARISSE: You rang?

SAM: Yeah, last Tuesday.

IRENE: Sam . . . !

CLARISSE *(bowing with a flourish):* My name is Clarisse, and it is my profound pleasure to welcome you to the Crossroads.

SAM: Right, right, great. We'd just like to go ahead and check in, please.

CLARISSE: Absolutely, sir. Just give me a moment to get my guest book, won't you?

(CLARISSE *dances to the counter with great style and skill, with several complex moves that lead her to the guest book. When she finally stops,* SAM *gives her a look as if to say, "Well?"* CLARISSE *smiles and commences dancing back to them, again taking a circuitously graceful route.* SAM *rolls his eyes. Presently she stops in front of them again.*)

EDDIE: Dude! Awesome!

IRENE: You are a wonderful dancer!

CLARISSE: Thank you. Very kind. The truth of it is, I just can't help myself.

SAM: Fascinating. Really. But our reservation is for a room, not for the ice follies. So if we could move this along, please?

CLARISSE *(dancing to* SAM*):* I am so sorry. Please forgive me.

SAM: All right.

CLARISSE: Say it, please.

SAM: Say what?

CLARISSE: Please say that you forgive me.

SAM: What?

CLARISSE: Please say that you forgive me. It's important for our relationship.

SAM: Whattayou . . . ? We don't have a relationship!

CLARISSE: See? That's what unforgiveness does.

IRENE: For heaven's sake, say it, Sam.

EDDIE: She needs to hear it.

SAM: Wha—? I—! Aw, you gotta be . . .

BRITTANY: Really, Daddy, how hard is it to say it?

SAM *(frowning):* Fine. I forgive you.

CLARISSE: Thank youuuuu!

(CLARISSE *takes off on another joyous dancing sequence around the room.* SAM *rubs his forehead like he's getting a migraine. Presently* CLARISSE *stops in front of them.*)

CLARISSE: Ooookee-dokee. What's the name?

IRENE: We're the D'Baquel family. And we're in gravy!

(*Uproarious laughter from* EDDIE, BRITTANY, *and especially* IRENE. *In fact,* IRENE *can't stop. She is nearly in tears when she finally gets composed.*)

IRENE: We always say that!

CLARISSE: Beg your pardon?

IRENE: We always say that! "We're the D'Baquel family, and we're in gravy."

CLARISSE: You're in gravy.

Sam: Gravy distributorship. Little gravy humor, there.

Clarisse: Oh.

Eddie: You ever heard of Gravy Grande? Well, that's us. My dad here founded the whole thing. Started 30 years ago with nothing but a ladle and three cubes of bouillon. Right, Dad?

Sam: That's right, son.

Clarisse: Impressive.

Brittany: He's one of the top gravy men you'll ever meet anywhere. In 1999, he was in the Top 10 in total gravy sales in his whole precinct!

Sam: It's true. "With Grande Gravy . . .

Family: Everything's Gravy!"

(Sam *pulls out a T-shirt with the slogan, "Everything's Gravy!"*)

Clarisse: Well, that is something. We are truly honored to have you, sir.

Sam: What can I say? Gravy is my life.

Eddie: Dad's grooming me to take over the empire someday.

Clarisse: Oh? What empire is that?

Eddie: The gravy empire! *(Pulls up his sweater to display his own T-shirt)* "Everything's Gravy!" *(Gives a thumbs up)*

Sam: Aw, Eddie! *(Groans)* For crying out loud!

Eddie: What?

Sam: Lookit here—You've got a stain on your T-shirt!

Eddie: I do?

Sam: If I've told you once, I've told you a thousand times! You cannot expect to sit on the gravy throne with a stain on your T-shirt!

(*With his finger,* SAM *dabs at the spot on the T-shirt. Then he decides to taste it.*)

SAM: Mmmmm! Sweet-n-Sour Southern Slop!

IRENE *(warmly):* One of your favorites!

OMA *(from offstage suddenly):* Oh . . . My . . . Goodness!

(OMA *sprints into the room.*)

OMA: O'magoodness! Ohhhh, m'goodness!

(*She continues on in this manner, with varying degrees of inflection and animation, just like* LEONARD *before her. At one point she even yells, "Oh, m'goodness!" and leaps into* EDDIE'S *arms. He and the other family members can do nothing but watch her.* CLARISSE *doesn't seem to notice, but continues preparing paperwork. Presently* OMA *exits, Oh-m'goodnessing all the way. A long beat as family considers what it has just seen.*)

BRITTANY: Excuse me.

CLARISSE: Yes?

BRITTANY: Um . . . is she . . . OK?

CLARISSE *(looking up):* Oh, yes. Much better.

(*Beat*)

SAM: Uh . . . much better than what?

CLARISSE: Much better than . . . before. *(Smile)* Now, Mr. D'Baquel. *(Dancing over to* SAM*)* May I ask how you heard about us?

IRENE: We received a free invitation. Sam thought it was junk mail.

SAM *(aside to* BRITTANY*):* And now I'm certain of it.

IRENE: It must've been part of some mass mailing. Everybody I know got one.

CLARISSE: Yes, we're in the middle of a major marketing push.

It's very exciting. Now your room will be down the hall and up the stairs . . .

SAM: Up the stairs?

CLARISSE: Just a couple of little stairs, Mr. D'Baquel.

SAM: More stairs . . . You people are going to be outside the earth's atmosphere here in a minute. In that case, you can tell your gardener/handyman/bellhop/Jake-of-all-trades that he absolutely can help me with my luggage.

CLARISSE: Oh, he'll be thrilled. *(Dances to the front door and calls out, sing-songy)* Oh, Jaaaaaaaake! Live bags here! Chop-chop! *(Giggles)*

(CLARISSE *dances back to the family, throwing in some unnecessary gymnastics along the way.*)

CLARISSE: He'll be right up.

SAM *(to* IRENE*)*: Make her stop doing that, please. I'm getting motion sickness.

CLARISSE: Now this evening, beginning at 7 o'clock right here in the lobby, we're inviting all our guests to a huge New Year's Eve party!

BRITTANY: Really?

EDDIE: Dude!

BRITTANY: Par-teee!

EDDIE: Paaar-tayyy!

BRITTANY *(in a cheer):* P-A-R-T-Y!
    You ain't got no alibi!
    Let's party!
    Uh, uh, let's party!

    Tell your mama you'll be late
    The Boogey Man has got a date!
    Party!
    Uh, uh, let's party!

(*She finishes with a flourish. She gets warm smiles and applause from her parents.*)

EDDIE (*looking for a little attention himself*): Parrr-tayyy!

BRITTANY: Parr-tay!

EDDIE: Parr-tayyy!

(EDDIE *begins getting quite funky, with moonwalks or other outrageous moves.*)

BRITTANY (*singing*): Go, brother! Go, brother!

EDDIE (*strutting around*): Parrr-tayyyy! Parr-tayyy! (*He grabs the soda can he brought in with him and smashes it against his head, sending soda everywhere.*) Arrrrrrggghhhh! (*Shakes his head to clear it and strikes an Egyptian pose*) To-gah! To-gah! To-gah!

(*Losing it now,* EDDIE *grabs a nearby tablecloth, ties it around himself like a toga and jumps up on the dining table.*)

EDDIE: To-gah! To-gah! To—

(*He stops in mid-toga when he catches his father's disapproving look.* EDDIE *suddenly realizes that everyone else is staring at him with concern. They hold their worried gaze for a long moment.*)

SAM (*aside, to* IRENE): I tell you, Irene, the gravy empire is in a lot of trouble.

EDDIE (*climbing down*): Uh . . . sorry, Dad.

(EDDIE *puts the tablecloth back on and begins to straighten it.*)

EDDIE: Forgive me.

SAM: Just fix the table.

EDDIE: Actually, Dad, I need to hear you say it.

SAM: Say what?

EDDIE: That you forgive me.

SAM (*exploding*): I'm not going to say that I forgive you! I'm going to say that you're a lunatic! *(Snotty mimicking)* "I need to hear you say it, Dad . . ."

EDDIE *(hurt):* You said it to Clarisse . . . !

SAM *(to* CLARISSE*):* Sorry. He was raised by wolves.

(CLARISSE *dances quickly up to* SAM.)

CLARISSE *(happily):* It's OK! I forgive you!

(CLARISSE *hugs* SAM *and dances away.* SAM *looks more baffled than ever.* JAKE *has reentered with a bellhop's cart and quietly begun to load* SAM'S *luggage onto it.)*

CLARISSE: Now, Mr. and Mrs. D'Baquel . . . please be advised that the party goes on until midnight.

SAM *(looking at his watch):* Yeah, OK. Midnight. I— *(tapping his watch)* Aw, look at this, Irene. My watch stopped working.

IRENE: Hmmm. Mine too.

SAM: Probably passed out from a lack of oxygen up here. *(To* CLARISSE.*)* Can you tell us how long we have until midnight?

CLARISSE *(dancing to* SAM, *stopping suddenly):* How long?

SAM: Uh . . . yeah. How long until midnight?

CLARISSE: Nobody really knows for sure.

SAM: Nobody knows? What do you mean? Nobody here knows what time it is?

CLARISSE: Well, Innkeeper Fred knows, of course.

SAM: Innkeeper Fred?

CLARISSE: Yes.

BRITTANY: He's the only one?

CLARISSE: That's right.

SAM: Well, let me ask you this, Miss Clerky Lady: How is anybody at your New Year's Party supposed to know when it's midnight?

CLARISSE: Oh, Innkeeper Fred will tell us.

SAM: Uh-huh. *(To* IRENE.*)* Innkeeper Fred will tell us! Thank you, that's a great comfort!

IRENE *(shrug):* I told you he was legendary.

CLARISSE *(dancing to* IRENE *excitedly):* You know Innkeeper Fred?

IRENE *(blushing):* I'm sort of a big fan.

SAM: Yes, yes, OK, we all know about the famous Innkeeper Fred. How he's known to millions and retailed more hamburgers to the starving nations of the world and saved the whales and whatever else. We can line up to salute him later. Is there anything else?

CLARISSE *(dancing back to counter):* Yes, sir. Here's your copy of the house rules. *(Dances back to* SAM *with a single sheet of paper.)* If you'll kindly look them over and sign.

(SAM, IRENE, *and* BRITTANY *look them over.* JAKE, *unnoticed by all but* EDDIE, *has meanwhile taken* SAM'S *bags to the door and begun heaving them over the railing, into the canyon below. He watches each one make the long fall, and we hear the distant impact.* EDDIE *grows increasingly alarmed, but is clearly torn about interrupting his father.)*

SAM *(looking at rules):* What's this here . . . ?

EDDIE: Um . . . Dad?

SAM: Hold on a second, son. *(To* CLARISSE.*)* This says that all breakfast service will stop after midnight.

CLARISSE: That's correct.

EDDIE: Hey, Dad, um, I really think—

SAM: I said hold on a second, Eddie! *(To* CLARISSE.*)* Well, how can you say there's no breakfast service after midnight? There'll be breakfast in the morning, won't there? I mean, this *is* a bed and breakfast . . .

27

CLARISSE *(shrug):* Innkeeper Fred's rules.

(EDDIE *has moved to the telescope and is looking down into the canyon with it.*)

EDDIE: Dad, sorry, I just—

SAM: Eddie, please! *(To* CLARISSE.*)* Listen, sister. Where I come from, we call that false advertising. If you don't serve breakfast after midnight, then this isn't a bed-and-breakfast at all, is it? Hoho, no! It's just a "bed," and that's very different from a bed-and-breakfast, wouldn't you say?

CLARISSE *(shrug):* Depends on your viewpoint, I suppose.

SAM *(scoff):* Depends on your viewpoint! Answer me this: Would you stay at a bed-and-breakfast that offered only a breakfast, but no bed? Huh? *(Proudly)* I think not!

CLARISSE: To Innkeeper Fred, I think bed-and-breakfast merely means that he can offer you wonderful rest and abundant food.

SAM: Hoho! But not after the clock strikes midnight!

CLARISSE: Uh, correct.

SAM: And who's the only one who knows when it's midnight? Innkeeper Fred! What a co-ink-a-dink!

IRENE: It is a little strange, Clarisse . . .

SAM: Look, lady. You think we haven't seen the same kind of stunts pulled in the gravy biz? Well, we have. And I have to tell you, I've got about half-a-mind to just up and leave, right now! Just take my family and my bags and head straight back down to the car.

EDDIE *(now at the door, peering down):* Dad . . . I think the bags have already headed straight back down.

SAM: What?

(SAM *rushes to the railing, and looks downward. He squints for a long moment and stands agape. He runs to the telescope, looks downward with it, and reacts in horror.*)

SAM: Aaaaaaauuugh! Wha—? Wha—? *(Turning back into the room)* What are my bags doing in a dusty heap at the bottom of the canyon?

(BRITTANY *and* IRENE *rush to the railing and look down.)*

SAM: You there! Bellhop guy! Didn't I ask you to take care of my bags?

JAKE: Yes, sir.

SAM *(pleading): And?*

JAKE: And I did, sir.

SAM: You call this taking care of the bags? Pitching them into space over a moon crater? What, you guys get a holiday bonus for every rattlesnake you pick off with a flying Sampsonite? Is that it?

JAKE: I didn't think you needed all that baggage, sir.

SAM: You wha—? Who asked you?

JAKE: No one, sir.

SAM: I—! I—! If I didn't need it, why would I bring it, you fruit loop! *(To* CLARISSE.*)* Is he for real?

CLARISSE *(dancing over to* SAM*):* So far as I know, sir. And you really don't need all of those things.

SAM: Says who? Oh, wait, wait, wait . . . just let me guess: Innkeeper Fred.

CLARISSE: That's right.

SAM: Uh-huh.

CLARISSE: He is legendary.

SAM: Yeah? Well, that's it. I demand to see him! *(To* JAKE.*)* You best start typing up a few resumes, pal. You're yesterday's gravy!

IRENE: Wasn't your laptop in there, honey?

SAM *(anguished):* My laptop! The quarterly gravy reports!

BRITTANY: Ooooo, and your recipe files too, Daddy.

SAM: My recipe files! The secrets of 31 gravy flavors, scattered into the wind!

EDDIE: Whoa, Dad . . . and what about your cell phone?

SAM: Aaaaaauuuggghhh! My cell phone! *(Sprints out the door)* I'm comin'! Hold on, Cell-ie! Daddy's comin'!

(Rest of the family stands staring at JAKE, *who stares back.)*

IRENE *(kindly):* Um . . . I hope you're not waiting around for a tip. . . .

(Lights down)

SCENE 2

(Lights up. As music continues, the room is full of partygoers, all of them moving in some fashion to the music. With his father absent, EDDIE *is dancing wildly up on the table again, egged on by some of the* GUESTS. IRENE *is looking out at the canyon through the telescope, and bopping to the beat.* CLARISSE *is dancing around the room as before, demonstrating for* BRITTANY, *who is trying to mimic her.* OMA, SABRINA, *and* LEONARD *are also in the party mix, and other members of the ensemble.* FRANKLIN'S *dancing, in large part, involves various forms of falling face-down on the floor.* JAKE *is mixing in and discretely picking through everyone's purses, backpacks, etc.*

Fade music, the GUESTS *segue out of dance and into animated conversation. Several are wearing party hats, etc.)*

EDDIE *(on dining table):* Paaaaar-tay!

*(*EDDIE *smashes another soda can on his head. He looks a little dazed.)*

IRENE *(looking through telescope at dancing* EDDIE*):* Eddie, honey . . . tuck in your shirt, please.

*(*EDDIE *does so.)*

IRENE *(still on telescope):* Thaaaat's better. Now, son, I'm not sure your father would approve of this kind of behavior. It's probably not befitting to the future king of gravy.

EDDIE *(talking to telescope):* I know it, Mom, but I just can't help it. I gotta, like, go with my own beat, you know? I gotta, like, make my own road! When the new king takes over, there'll be no more Gravy Grande! There'll only be . . . *(dancing "the monkey" or something similar)* . . . Gravy Groovy!

(The front door slams open and SAM *reappears, looking more haggard and puffing even harder than before. He is loaded down again by his luggage, though it looks dirtier and more torn up now.)*

IRENE *(going to him):* Oh, Sam. Thank heavens. I was getting worried about you!

SAM *(gasping for breath):* So was I.

IRENE: Did you find your laptop? And your cell phone?

SAM *(nodding wearily):* Yeah . . . I found them, all right. Phone was even still ringing.

IRENE: You're kidding! Who was it?

SAM *(nodding to* JAKE*):* Sir Frankenbutler over there. Wanted to know if I needed a hand with my bags.

*(*SABRINA *has quietly approached* SAM *and* IRENE, *looking not at them, but into the distance with a wide-eyed look.)*

SABRINA: Whooooaaaaaaaa!

*(*SAM *watches her carefully, then gives a polite smile.)*

SAM *(patronizing):* Hi. How ya doin'. *(Looking at* SABRINA, *but talking to* IRENE.*)* Nice. This is very nice.

SABRINA *(moving to their other side, still looking into distance):* I mean, like . . . whoa!

SAM *(fake kindness):* Yes . . . yes, absolutely. I couldn't agree more.

*(*SABRINA *moves on.* SAM'S *demeanor changes immediately.)*

SAM *(through his teeth)*: I blame you, Irene, I blame you completely! I could've been basting on the deck of a cruise ship in Acapulco right now! Instead I'm the guest of honor at Barnum & Bailey's Mile-High Asylum!

BRITTANY: Daddyyyyyy! *(Bouncing up and giving him a big hug)*

SAM: Ow . . . ow . . . hi, sweetie. *(Wearily)* Are you having a good time?

BRITTANY: Oh, yes, Daddy! There's lots of boys!

SAM: Good. Good. I'm glad there's lots of boys.

BRITTANY *(perky)*: I'm not! I'd like to see them all staked to the ground in the baking desert sun and then run over by a stampede of large, angry bison with mad cow disease!

SAM *(staring hard at* IRENE*)*: Did I mention that I'm blaming you?

BRITTANY: Oh, Daddy—guess what? Clarisse is teaching me how to dance everywhere like she does!

CLARISSE *(dancing over to* SAM*)*: Indeed, I am, Mr. D'Baquel. And may I say that it is a profound pleasure to do so. *(Dancing to* IRENE.*)* That girl of yours has limitless potential, I tell you! Limitless!

SAM: She sure does have limitless potential, and I'll thank you to stay away from it!

IRENE: Sam . . .

BRITTANY: Oh, Daddy, it's so awesome! Can I show you what I've learned so far?

SAM: No.

BRITTANY: No?

IRENE *(nudging* SAM, *sing-song)*: Su-ppor-tive . . .

SAM: No . . . chance in the world I would miss it, angel. Show me.

BRITTANY: Well . . . I'm not very good yet, but . . . OK!

(BRITTANY *positions herself to dance, and* CLARISSE *excitedly helps her.*)

CLARISSE: Now, remember, Brittany. Your dancing must spring up naturally out of the deep joy that lives within you!

BRITTANY: Got it! Deep joy! Deep within me! Here we go! Ready?

IRENE: Ready!

SAM (*less enthusiastically*): Uh, ready.

(BRITTANY *sets to dance across the room. She gets a few graceful steps before crashing in a bad way, possibly taking out other* GUESTS *and furniture with her.* SAM *and* IRENE *run to her.*)

SAM: Princess! Are you all right?

BRITTANY (*rising hurriedly*): I'm fine, Daddy, I'm fine. (*Preening her hair and clothes*) My deep joy must've gotten the best of me!

EDDIE: Maybe the zit on her forehead threw her off balance . . .

(SAM *glares at* EDDIE, *who shrinks back.*)

IRENE: Don't you worry, dear. That was still very beautiful.

BRITTANY: Do you think so?

SAM: Oh, absolutely, princess. Most people, when they crack their head on a table leg and wipe out three bystanders, look totally clumsy! But you made it look elegant!

BRITTANY: Well, that's good. I wouldn't want people to think I was some kind of clod or something! Not that I think there's anything wrong with people who are clods, of course. I wouldn't want anyone to say that I was, like, clod prejudiced, or anything like that, because I'm not. Some of my very best friends are clods! Well, not my closest friends, of course, but . . . you know what I mean . . .

CLARISSE: Yes . . .

BRITTANY: —and it's not like I haven't known some clumsy people, you know? I mean, I've known some clumsy people, believe me!

CLARISSE: Uh-huh.

BRITTANY: I could say things to them, but I don't. You know, because if there's one thing I don't want to be, it's one of those really mean people. You know?

CLARISSE *(listening intently)*: Oh, yeah.

BRITTANY: I mean, who likes mean people? You know? Nobody! I know I sure don't.

CLARISSE: Uh-huh.

BRITTANY: And for me to not like mean people, and then to be a mean person . . . well, that would be, like, hypothetical, don't you think?

(CLARISSE *blinks a moment.*)

CLARISSE: Hypocritical.

BRITTANY: Hyp . . . ? Oh, wow, did I say hypothetical? *(Giggle)* Woops. My bad! Now, see, a mean person would take that and make some stupid joke about cheerleaders being dumb or whatever. But a nice person—like me . . . like you!—a nice person would realize it was just a mistake. That's all! A little mistake! And everybody makes mistakes! Right?

CLARISSE: Right.

BRITTANY: Right. Just like sometimes everybody crashes headlong into tables . . . right?

(SAM *has pulled* IRENE *to one side.*)

SAM: Irene, please. I mean, I'm OK with getting pretty weird on New Year's Eve, all right? I am. But this place is like Mardi Gras on steroids or something.

IRENE: Oh, come on, grumpy pants. You're just tired. Now set your things down. I'll go get you a glass of punch.

SAM: Thank you.

(IRENE *departs.* SAM *begins unloading his bags, taking a long time to do so. He is just about free of them when he notices* JAKE *standing by, watching him. Warily* SAM *eyes him for a moment, then slowly and painstakingly picks up all the bags again and moves to the sofa. He plops down heavily with all his stuff, sitting right next to* OMA. SAB-RINA *reappears next to* SAM, *still looking into the distance, but grabbing* SAM *by the arm this time.*)

SABRINA: Whooooaaaaa! *(Astonished)* Whoa!

(She moves on. SAM *sighs, reaches into his pocket for aspirin, and pops a couple. He taps* OMA *on the shoulder.)*

SAM: Pardon me. Would you know how long it is until midnight?

OMA *(kindly)*: Sorry. Nobody really knows. *(She looks at him carefully.)* Hey, don't I know you from somewhere?

SAM: You jumped into my son's arms like an escaped mental patient this afternoon.

OMA: Right, right!

SAM *(extending hand)*: I'm Sam D'Baquel. And I'm in gravy.

OMA *(sizing him up)*: I can tell.

SAM: And you are?

OMA: Oma.

SAM: Oma . . .

OMA: Goodness.

SAM *(eye roll)*: Oma Goodness. Naturally.

OMA: And are you enjoying your stay so far, Sam?

SAM: Oh, sure. You know, if you don't count my being the victim of a sadistic weirdo.

OMA: You mean, masochistic.

SAM: Beg pardon.

OMA: You said "sadistic," but that's when somebody else inflicts it upon you. Masochistic is the right word for when you inflict it on yourself.

(SAM *sits confused. Then he notices* JAKE *right behind him, unzipping one of his duffel bags and reaching in.*)

SAM *(jumping up):* Hey, get away from there, man! Get your mitts off, dude! *(Pointing)* I'll press charges!

JAKE: My apologies.

SAM: What do you think you're doing?!

JAKE: Cleaning it out for you.

SAM: I do not need you to clean it out for me, you freakazoid!

JAKE: I think you do.

SAM: Well, thanks very much for your opinion, Monsieur Space Cadet. But I'd say you've done enough damage! Already had to wrestle my laptop back from a bunch of bad-attitude gila monsters, thanks to you! So get away! Stand over there! (JAKE *takes a few steps away.*) Further! *(A few more)* Now that's the distance I want you, comprende? No closer!

(SAM *sits back down.* OMA *hasn't even noticed the commotion. He nudges her.*)

SAM: Believe this guy? Earlier today he took all my luggage and threw it into the great abyss out there.

OMA: I know! He did it with mine too!

(*She turns back to her conversation.* SAM *is confused a moment. He taps her again.*)

SAM: He did?

OMA: Did what?

SAM: Threw all your stuff into the great abyss!

OMA: Oh, yeah! Isn't it awesome?

(*She turns back to her conversation.* SAM *sits confused another moment, and taps her again.*)

SAM: I beg your pardon, but no, it is not awesome. It completely trashed my wardrobe, scattered my business files, and crushed a half-dozen personal electronic devices! And let's not even talk about my supply of "Everything's Gravy" T-shirts!

OMA: OK! Let's not!

(*She turns back to conversation.* SAM *is flummoxed. He taps her once more.*)

SAM: Excuse me. Sorry. So . . . didn't all your stuff get completely smashed?

OMA: Yeah, it did! (*Excitedly*) Smashed! Smashed right to powder! Unnhhh! Unbelievable! Incredible!

SAM: OK. I give. What is so incredible about that?

OMA: You don't know?

SAM: Well . . . I mean . . . no, I don't.

OMA (*to* LEONARD): He doesn't know!

(LEONARD *gives a baby shriek; he's trying to suppress it.*)

OMA: He really doesn't know! (*To* SAM.) You don't know!

SAM: I think we've established that, yeah.

OMA: Innkeeper Fred, man!

(*An excited squeak from* LEONARD.)

SABRINA: Whoa!

SAM: Innkeeper Fred.

OMA: Yes, yes! Innkeeper Fred!

SAM: Where?

OMA: Everywhere, man! Innkeeper Freeeeed!

SAM: OK. What about him?

OMA: What about him? What about him? Oh, my goodness!

(LEONARD *lets out a full shriek.*)

OMA: O'magoodness!!

SABRINA: Whoa!

(OMA, SABRINA, *and* LEONARD *begin trading exclamations.*)

OMA *(leaping up on table):* Hey, everybody! Innkeeper Fred!

(*The whole place, except for the four family members, begins excited exclamations.* CLARISSE *begins dancing around, extra joyously.* SAM *stands at the middle of it all, looking totally miserable for 10 or 15 seconds.*)

SAM *(finally):* All right, knock it off!

(*Everyone stops except* FRANKLIN, *who remains stretched out facedown on the ground, quivering as though he's being electrocuted. Everyone stares at him for a moment.*)

SAM: What's this guy doing?

EDDIE: Dude, I'm not sure, but I think it's . . . The Worm!

(*He throws himself on the ground and begins quivering uncontrollably.*)

BRITTANY: Wheeee!

(BRITTANY *cartwheels and joins in the Worm.*)

EDDIE: Parrrr-tayyyy!

BRITTANY: Parrrr-tayyyyy!

(IRENE *walks up and holds out a glass of punch for* SAM. *He continues staring at his children quivering on the ground.*)

SAM *(taking glass):* Whatever this is, Irene, it can't possibly be strong enough. *(Gulps it down)* Hokay, family meeting!

(*He grabs* EDDIE *and* BRITTANY *each by an arm, and the four D'Baquels move downstage. The party resumes quietly behind them.*)

BRITTANY: What's up, Daddy?

SAM: Here's what's up. If you ask me, I think—

(He stops because he suddenly notices JAKE, *who has joined their family huddle and is listening intently.* SAM's *threatening look makes* JAKE *realize he's not welcome;* JAKE *retreats to a more peripheral position.)*

SAM *(to family):* All right. What's really going on here?

EDDIE: Where?

SAM: Here! This place! Kooksville, USA!

IRENE: What do you mean, Sam? We're all having a wonderful time.

SAM: Yeah? Well, I smell a rat.

EDDIE *(shrug):* Call housekeeping.

SAM *(ignoring him):* I tell you, something doesn't feel right to me. Too many things just don't add up.

BRITTANY: Like what, Daddy?

SAM: First of all . . . have any of you, in the entire time we've been here, seen this Innkeeper Fred guy, even for an instant?

EDDIE *(shrug):* No.

(The others shrug and shake their heads.)

SAM: OK. And think about it. Do we actually have any tangible evidence that this character even exists?

BRITTANY: Who? Innkeeper Fred?

SAM: Shhhh! *(Looking around)* Don't say his name too loud! It overexcites the natives.

IRENE: You don't think Innkeeper Fred exists? Oh, Sam . . . please, honey! What kind of silliness is that?

SAM: Irene. Ask yourself this question. If this guy really existed—if he were a real person—don't you think that somebody somewhere would call the man just plain Fred?

IRENE: What?

SAM: Innkeeper Fred, Innkeeper Fred! Who goes by a name like that? Would you go by a name like that? Hey, look! It's Housewife Irene! I believe I'll go over and play bridge with Housewife Irene! After she gets home from the carpool with her two kids, Cheerleader Brittany and . . . Slacker Ed!

EDDIE *(pulling knit cap over his face, posing like a wrestler):* How about, Big Ed the Mangler?

IRENE: Honey, look. They talk about Innkeeper Fred right here in the brochure.

SAM: Slick marketing, Irene, nothing more. I can claim anything in a brochure. We do it all the time in the gravy business. Our Gravy No. 28? Sassy Sushi Saucy? People don't even realize that it's exactly the same formula as our Gravy No. 6.

IRENE: Smoking Mojave lava? No!

SAM: Believe it.

EDDIE: Well, why don't you just make one flavor out of them, Dad?

SAM: Because, Einstein . . . then we'd only have 30 flavors, wouldn't we? Duhhh!

BRITTANY: I still don't understand. What's that got to do with Innkeeper Fred?

SAM: Shhhh! *(Cupping her mouth)* The name! You saw what happened a minute ago. This place looked like a jailbreak from an ant farm!

EDDIE: Right on . . .

SAM: Listen to me, all of you. I'll bet everything I have that Innkeeper Fred is Innkeeper Fraud! A complete myth. He doesn't exist any more than Sassy Sushi Saucy does.

IRENE: Well, why would they put him in the brochure, Sam?

SAM: It's all a ploy, Irene! Don't you see? Why do you think they send out free invitations—huh? Get people believing that there's this magical Innkeeper Fred guy, and that he's this famous icon that anybody would naturally want to be around. And then, when the people start coming from miles around . . . uh-huh . . . You put your creepy bellhop in position to get his hands on their precious luggage!

IRENE: Honestly, Sam. What, do you think all of these wonderful people here are in on the plot? They obviously believe there's a real Innkeeper Fred.

SAM: They're the victims, Irene! Don't you see? They're brainwashed, is what it is. How else to explain the fact that every single one of them is absolutely whacked!

BRITTANY: Whacked, yes. But, Daddy, brainwashed?

SAM: Yes, sweetie! And we will be too, if we're not careful!

IRENE: Sam, you're just being paranoid. If you want to know about Innkeeper Fred, why don't you just ask Clarisse?

SAM: No, no! She's . . . *(looking around suspiciously)* one of them.

IRENE: Who?

SAM: Who do you think? The conspirators! She's probably the mastermind behind the whole thing!

(They all gaze at CLARISSE, *who's doing rather bizarre dance moves off by herself. Not exactly looking like a criminal mastermind.)*

IRENE: Oh, now, stop this, Sam. *(Calling to* CLARISSE.*)* Clarisse? Could you come over here for a moment, please?

CLARISSE: Certainly!

*(*CLARISSE *dances over to them.)*

SAM *(as she's coming, through his teeth)*: I don't need to talk to Clarisse!

CLARISSE *(arriving)*: Yes? How may I be of service?

IRENE: Well. *(Smiling)* Sam here has some questions about—

SAM: No, I don't!

IRENE: Oh, yes, you do. *(To CLARISSE.)* Yes, he does.

SAM: No, I don't. No questions. I'm good. *(Trying to shoo her)* As you were. Thank you.

CLARISSE: Is anything wrong?

IRENE: Actually . . .

SAM: No! Nothing wrong!

EDDIE: Aw, don't be shy, Dad! Ask her!

SAM: I am not being shy. I do not have a problem. Thank you, Chartreuse.

CLARISSE: Clarisse.

SAM: Whatever.

IRENE: Sam! *(Under her breath, pulling him aside)* Why don't you just come out and ask her about—

SAM: Don't say it.

IRENE: Say what?

SAM: That name.

IRENE: What name?

SAM *(smiling at CLARISSE)*: You know. That name. The one we're not saying.

EDDIE *(to CLARISSE)*: He's afraid a wild ant farm is going to break out.

CLARISSE: Really? I used to be afraid that fiddler crabs were going to carry me away in my sleep.

BRITTANY: That's awful!

IRENE: You poor thing!

CLARISSE: Yes. Every time my family went out for seafood, I'd go into hysteria.

SAM *(losing it):* Who cares? Can we get back to our family meeting, please?

IRENE: Honey, you're losing it.

SAM: I am not losing it!

EDDIE: Maybe he's got Inverted Bi-Polar Maiden Complex.

(SAM *stares at him.*)

SAM: I do not have Inverted Bi-Polar Maiden Complex! There is no such thing as Inverted Bi-Polar Maiden Complex! OK! There is no such thing as Inverted Bi-Polar Maiden Complex, there is no such thing as Sassy Sushi Saucy, and there is no such thing as Innkeeper Fred!

(CLARISSE *gasps.* SAM *stops, realizing what he's just done.*)

CLARISSE: Innkeeper Fred?

SAM: No . . .

OMA: Oh, my goodness!

CLARISSE *(happily):* Hey, everyone! Innkeeper Fred!

(LEONARD *shrieks. Music kicks up. The* GUESTS *begin to run around crazily again.*)

SAM: Wait a minute! Wait a minute! I did not say "Innkeeper Fred!" I said . . . I said . . . "My Beekeeper's Dead!"

(*It's too late. The* GUESTS *are having another joyous outburst to the music.* SAM *ends up ducking them, and crawling around them, and trying to negotiate his way through them.*)

SAM *(rubbing his migraine):* It's a nightmare. That's what it is. Just a nightmare. *(Looking around at the chaos)* A really noisy and stupid nightmare! Yo, Clarisse! *(Nods her over)* You think there's, like, any way we could keep these people just a little bit under control? I mean, really! Some of us are on vacation here!

CLARISSE: I'm sorry, Mr. D'Baquel! It's just . . . Innkeeper Fred!

SAM: I know! Innkeeper Fred! Whoopee! Would somebody mind telling me what the big deal is?

CLARISSE: He's, like, the greatest ever!

SAM *(losing it):* He's a stinking innkeeper!

(More lunacy from the other GUESTS, *now joined in full joy by* EDDIE, IRENE, *and* BRITTANY. SAM *keeps trying to get to his family members to stop them, but keeps getting cut off or frustrated in various ways. At one point,* IRENE *may even lay across the dining table, use a flower vase as a microphone, and mime some words like a piano lounge singer.* SAM *grabs her and drags her off to one side as the music wraps up.)*

SAM: All right, that does it. I'm not just going to stand by and watch while innocent people get duped and deceived. Sometime before midnight tonight, Sam D'Baquel is going to have a serious head-on collision with Mr. Innkeeper Fred! *(Beat, steely stare)* Oh, yeah. This is where the gravy meets the road, baby!

(Lights out)

End Act I

Act II

SCENE 1

(*Spot up on* BRITTANY, *sitting alone in her cheerleader's outfit on the sofa. Dark music plays behind her. In a stark contrast to the frivolity of the first act, she is sitting blankly with her hair askew. She raises one arm slowly and regards her bare forearm. Then she raises her other hand to reveal a large kitchen knife and pulls it slowly to her wrist. She begins to move with the music, the edge of the knife playing on her wrist.*

She throws the knife down on the music crash and begins a wild, strobe dance of no control, chaos, and confusion. In this piece she may also be pursued and harassed by dark demons. At some point, JAKE *enters, takes in the scene, and casts/throws off the demons, one by one. With the last* DEMON *cast,* JAKE *raises a powerful hand slowly—and with it raises* BRITTANY *from her place on the floor.* DEMONS *exit. Fade music. As it ends,* BRITTANY *is unaware of the presence that has protected her and stayed her hand. She returns to the sofa, where she began.*

Lights up. Party music, and the room comes to life. JAKE *discreetly withdraws.* BRITTANY *quickly stashes the knife and pulls herself back into the moment. After a few moments of this, fade down music.*)

EDDIE (*dancing wildly*): This place is rocking, man! (*Nudges* FRANKLIN *nearby.*) Hey, how long 'til midnight?

FRANKLIN: Nobody knows, man!

EDDIE: Nobody?

FRANKLIN: Nobody but Innkeeper Fred! Just gotta be ready when it comes, man! (*Pointing offstage*) Look! That dude's making balloon animals! Let's go! (*Noticing* EDDIE'S *hesitation.*) What's the matter, man?

EDDIE: I had a balloon animal once, when I was five. (*Sadly*) It got hit by a car.

FRANKLIN: Man, I'm sorry. C'mon, I'll get you another one.

EDDIE *(happy again):* OK! *(They sprint offstage together.)*

OMA: Hey, everybody! I know! Let's play charades! *(A cheer goes up and they all gather 'round.)* Brittany, you first!

BRITTANY: Uh . . . OK!

(Wiping the last of her tears from her face, she goes up before the crowd.)

BRITTANY: All right, here we go. It's a famous movie character! *(Holds up one finger)*

OMA: One word . . .

(The charades game continues on in mime as SAM bursts through the door. He is carrying his luggage yet again—even more tattered—and really looking bushed. He stares daggers at JAKE.) IRENE *(approaching):* What, again?

SAM *(wheeze):* Guy's driving me crazy, Irene. Let down your guard for an instant and he's got your stuff flying over the edge. *(Gasp, gasp)* If I could lift my arms, I'd rip out his spleen right here.

IRENE: Now, Sam, maybe it's not his fault. It could be something genetic, you know.

Sam: Yeah, yeah. *(Unloading laptop again)* Poor slob was born with the chuck-your-suitcase-into-oblivion gene. *(Pant, pant)* Parents were probably airline baggage handlers.

IRENE: Oh, Sam.

SAM: Don't "Oh, Sam" me. He pitched some of your stuff too. I hauled it back up here for you.

(He produces a couple of IRENE'S bags.)

IRENE *(taken back):* You . . . what?

SAM: No need to thank me, pooky-lips. You hitch your wagon to the king of gravy, and he's gonna make sure that everything's gravy for you. Here you go.

IRENE *(staring at her luggage):* You . . . didn't have to do that,

Sam. I mean, I realized that he'd taken it from me and thrown it away, of course. But I thought . . . well, I don't know . . . maybe I'd just see what it was like to travel light for a while.

SAM *(scoff):* Travel light! Highly overrated, darlin', believe me. Here, hold still and I'll get you saddled up again.

(He begins to load her bags onto her back again. She sags noticeably with each additional burden.)

SAM: There we are! Now that's the Irene I've always known and loved!

(SAM swats her on the backpack and nearly knocks her over, she's so teetery. EDDIE appears with a pillowcase over his head, dancing wildly.)

EDDIE *(howling):* Parrr-taaayyy!

(He smashes another soda can on his pillowcased head. SAM steps over to EDDIE and stares at him.)

EDDIE: Paaarr-taaayyyy!

(SAM pulls the pillowcase off EDDIE'S head.)

EDDIE: Paaaar—! *(He stops short when he sees SAM.)* Paaar, paaar, par . . . pardon me, sir, aren't you the famous founder of Gravy Grande?

SAM: Cute. That's very cute.

EDDIE *(slumping):* Sorry, Dad. Sir.

SAM: Are you ever gonna grow up, Eddie? Huh? Act like a respectable adult? What, you wanna end up like these people? Is that it?

EDDIE: I . . . well . . . I mean, no. I guess.

SAM: You think people respect a man because he can smash a can on his head?

FRANKLIN: I do!

SAM: Aw, shut up. Let me tell you something, Eddie. People respect a man who takes control of his life and circumstances. They respect a man who displays at least a passing semblance of intelligence.

EDDIE: You're right, Dad. I know you're right.

SAM: You don't see your younger sister acting like an idiotic moron, do you? No, she's got herself together.

OMA *(with the charades crowd):* Pollyanna!

BRITTANY: Yes! Yes! That's my charade!

(A cheer goes up)

OMA: Good one, good one! All right, who's next? Sam?

SAM *(curtly):* I don't play charades.

OMA: Aw, you're missing out! How about you, Eddie?

(EDDIE looks meekly at his father.)

EDDIE: Naw . . . naw, I don't think I play charades, either.

CROWD: Awww . . . C'mon! . . . (etc.)

(CROWD begins looking for new clue-giver. JAKE has stepped up next to IRENE.)

JAKE: Take your baggage for you?

IRENE *(sadly):* No . . . no, I'd better hold onto them this time.

JAKE: You sure?

(IRENE shrugs and smiles sadly at him.)

OMA: Irene!

CROWD: Yeah, Irene! (etc.)

OMA: Come on . . . your turn at charades!

IRENE: Um . . . all right.

(IRENE *moves to the front of the charades crowd, still carrying her luggage.*)

IRENE: It's a TV show character. *(Holds up two fingers)*

OMA: Two words! First word . . .

(*Everything freezes. Dark instrumental music in the background. Presently both* EDDIE *and* IRENE *begin to move slowly while the others stay frozen. They are speaking in their own worlds, unaware of one another or anyone else.*)

EDDIE: You want me to play charades? Yeah, I'll play.

IRENE: I'll play.

EDDIE: I've played charades all my life. All my life!

IRENE: For years.

EDDIE: All my life!

IRENE *(head down)*: All my life.

EDDIE: Loving son.

IRENE: Picture-perfect mom.

EDDIE: Obedient son!

IRENE: Happy homemaker.

EDDIE: It's all a lie!

IRENE: It's not entirely a lie . . .

EDDIE: It's all a lie!

IRENE *(resigned)*: It's all a lie.

(JAKE *begins to move slowly in the background, first towards* IRENE.)

EDDIE: Yeah, I've played charades. *(Whirls to* SAM.*)* Pretended that you loved me!

IRENE *(removing vodka bottle and glass from her luggage)*: Pretended like it wasn't a problem.

EDDIE: Pretended like I respected you.

IRENE: Pretended like everything was fine.

EDDIE: Pretended like I wanted to be just like you. *(Beat)* Well, maybe I wasn't pretending then.

IRENE: Pretended like I could handle it. Pretended like I could quit anytime I wanted.

EDDIE *(pulling baseball bat from his luggage):* Pretended like you never hurt me.

(JAKE *begins to move toward* EDDIE.)

IRENE: Pretended like it never hurt anybody.

EDDIE *(sizing up laptop angrily):* Pretended like I was more important to you than your stupid business. Pretended like you thought about me when you were gone all the time. Pretended like you would come back and keep your promises.

IRENE: It was all a lie.

EDDIE *(gripping bat tighter):* It was all a lie!

IRENE: I hate myself. *(Returning bottle to her bag)*

(EDDIE *whirls quickly on his dad again.*)

EDDIE: I hate you!

(*He draws back the angry baseball bat and is about to shatter the laptop, but* JAKE *touches the bat and stops him. Fade down dark music; fade up party music. Lights up on all. Party comes back to life.* JAKE *quietly exits.* IRENE *and* EDDIE, *both a little shaken up, return to the moment.*)

OMA: June Cleaver!

IRENE *(forcing a smile):* Yes.

(A cheer goes up.)

BRITTANY: Good one, Mom! Wow, you did that really excellently!

IRENE: Years of practice, honey. Years of practice.

SAM *(plopped on the sofa):* Hey, where's the TV? Wasn't there a TV here?

BRITTANY: There was one . . .

(They all scout around for a minute.)

EDDIE: You know, I actually think I saw it on the baggage cart . . .

SAM: What . . . ? Why in the world . . . Uh-oh, wait a minute! You know what that means! If you want to watch *American Idol* tonight, you better put a trampoline down in the parking lot. Because our Babbling Bellhop has voted that baby off the island.

EDDIE: Where is that dude, anyway?

SAM: Maybe the luggage had an uprising and decided to throw him over the side.

(JAKE steps back into the room.)

JAKE: Friends and guests. I have been asked by my dad to inform you that . . . it's almost midnight.

(LEONARD begins shrieking, OMA begins "O'magoodness"ing, SABRINA begins "Whoa"ing, and bedlam breaks out. SAM shakes his head in resignation.)

SAM *(finally):* All right already! *(They all stop. He turns to IRENE.)* You know, if they just had the TV plugged in to Dick Clark, like normal people on New Year's Eve, we could all come back from Planet Bizarro here.

JAKE: Everything OK, sir?

SAM *(continuing):* Times Square. That's all I'm asking. Big apple dropping down. Thousands of people packed in like sardines, hollering like bloodthirsty cannibals and drinking themselves into a stupor in order to celebrate the turning of a calendar page. See? Normalcy. Reality. That's what we need a little more of here.

(JAKE *stares at him for a long moment.*)

JAKE: Can I help you with that baggage, sir?

SAM *(flipping):* No, you cannot help me with my baggage! What is it with you, anyway? Some kind of obsessive-compulsive suitcase disorder or something? What do I gotta do to keep you from grabbing my stuff and throwing it over the side?

JAKE *(shrug):* Stop bringing it back up.

(SAM *gives him a long, reproving look.*)

JAKE: Well, think about it. Wouldn't that be easier?

SAM: Look, it's my stuff. OK? My stuff. I brought it here, it's my stuff, and I want it here.

JAKE: No, you don't.

SAM: Yes, I do!

JAKE: You really don't.

SAM: Of course I do!

JAKE: You think you want it . . .

SAM: I think that because I do!

JAKE: . . . but trust me, you really don't.

(SAM *spits and sputters in a near-seizure.*)

SAM: I—! Ooo—! Uh—! You know, this place makes the Cartoon Channel look like a poetry reading! If midnight ever does come . . . *(stops suddenly)* wait a minute. Wait . . . what did you mean by that crack you just made? Your dad told you it was almost midnight? I thought the all-powerful Innkeeper Fred was the only one who knew when the clock was going to strike 12.

JAKE: He is. That's him.

SAM: That's . . . ?

JAKE: Mmmm-hmmm.

SAM: Innkeeper Fred is your . . .

JAKE: Father. That's right.

SAM *(laughing hard):* Yeah! I'll bet he is!

JAKE: Why is that so hard to believe?

SAM: Why? Well, for starters: I don't think our legendary innkeeper would make his son into a piddly doorman.

JAKE *(shrug):* Well . . . I'd rather be a doorman in the house of the—

SAM: Look. Pal. Junior. What do you think—that I fell off the gravy boat yesterday? Just give it up, man, OK? These other yokels may buy your act, but I'm hip to what's going on here. I know there is no Innkeeper Fred.

JAKE: You do?

SAM: Yes, I do. The guy's a myth. A fable, used by people like you to leverage and control and exploit other people.

JAKE: You know this.

SAM: I'd bet my life on it.

JAKE: Yes, that's exactly what I'm afraid of.

SAM: If there is an Innkeeper Fred, where is he? Huh? I haven't seen him yet.

JAKE: Maybe you've seen him but haven't recognized him.

SAM: Uh-huh. Right. And maybe the world is made of petrified Spam.

JAKE *(gesturing to party crowd):* They've seen him.

SAM: Them? Who, the barrel of monkeys over there? They are clearly escapees from some haywire stem-cell experiment.

JAKE: They act that way because of Innkeeper Fred.

SAM: Innkeeper Fred.

JAKE: They've seen him. *(Shrug)* It changes you.

SAM: They haven't seen anything! And if they say they have, it's only because their imaginations are in turbo time-warp.

JAKE: You think Innkeeper Fred is all in their imaginations?

SAM: Yes, I do.

(Fade up dark music again. Everyone freezes but JAKE *and* SAM. JAKE *approaches the party crowd.)*

JAKE *(gesturing to* OMA*):* This one was a prostitute when she got here. Now she's not. *(Gesturing to* FRANKLIN.*)* This one was bitter and critical of everything and everyone. Now he's not. *(Gesturing to* LEONARD.*)* This one had left his wife and children and run off with his Internet lover. Now he's home. *(Gesturing to others.)* This one was wracked by years of grieving, that one was pouring his life into material things. *(Beat)* This one was consumed by loneliness. Now they're not.

SAM *(after a moment):* So?

JAKE: So, that's a pretty good imagination, wouldn't you say?

*(*SAM *stands staring.)*

JAKE: Let me ask you something, Sam. Why did you come here?

SAM: Pffh. I sure didn't want to, I can tell you that.

JAKE: You didn't.

SAM: No way. On the cruise ship to Acapulco, they leave your stinkin' luggage alone.

JAKE: I think you did want to come here, Sam.

SAM: Yeah, well, you're wrong. For some people, this whole Innkeeper Fred thing might float their boat. That's fine. But it's not for me. It's not for the D'Baquel family.

JAKE: Mmmm. Are you sure?

SAM: Yeah, I'm su—

(SAM *stops short, as* BRITTANY *turns out slowly, again isolated in her own world. She moves downstage with a duffel and pulls the kitchen knife from it.*)

SAM *(stunned)*: Princess . . .

(IRENE *now turns out slowly, moves downstage with a suitcase, and pulls the vodka bottle out.*)

SAM: Irene . . . !

(EDDIE *turns out slowly, moves downstage with his backpack, pulls out the baseball bat.*)

SAM *(confused)*: Eddie?

(*With his cart,* JAKE *moves slowly behind* BRITTANY, *who is holding the knife at her wrist.*)

JAKE: Excuse me, miss. May I help you with your baggage?

(BRITTANY *wavers.*)

JAKE *(more gently)*: Excuse me, miss. May I help you with your sorrow and your anxiety?

(BRITTANY *slowly hands over the knife and falls to her knees.*)

JAKE *(to* IRENE*)*: Excuse me, ma'am. May I help you with your addiction and your lies?

(IRENE *slowly hands over the bottle and falls to her knees.*)

JAKE *(to* EDDIE*)*: Excuse me, sir. May I help you with your pain and your anger?

(EDDIE *slowly hands over the baseball bat and falls to his knees.* JAKE *approaches* SAM, *who is looking wide-eyed and scared.*)

JAKE: Excuse me, sir. May I help you with your baggage?

SAM *(quickly)*: No.

JAKE: Excuse me, sir. May I help you with your doubts . . . and your deep, hidden fears . . . and your guilt . . .

SAM: What are you talking about? I don't have any of those things!

JAKE: No? *(Nodding to* SAM'S *luggage.)* What do you have in there?

SAM: None of your business!

JAKE: What do you think you're hiding, Sam?

SAM: I'm not hiding anything! You know, that's it. I'm outta here! *(Picking up luggage to go)* Leave me alone! Leave my family alone!

(He has turned to go, but then stops, seeming confused. He turns back to JAKE.*)*

SAM: Hey . . . what'd you say your name was?

JAKE: I think you know my name, Sam. And you know my father's name too. *(Beat)* Are you absolutely certain I can't help you with that?

*(*SAM *is softened for a moment, but hardens again.)*

SAM: No. I told you—I don't play charades!

(Lights down)

SCENE 2

(Lights up. Fade down music. CLARISSE *is behind the desk,* JAKE *standing sentry at the door, and* SAM *alone in the middle of the room.)*

SAM: Hey! Where'd everybody go?

CLARISSE *(not looking up)*: Party's over, Mr. D'Baquel.

SAM: What, just like that? How much longer to midnight?

CLARISSE: You don't want to know. Here's your bill.

SAM: My what?

CLARISSE: Your bill, Mr. D'Baquel.

SAM: What're you talking about, my bill? I thought we had a free gift certificate to be here!

CLARISSE: Oh, you do, sir. But there's still damages that must be paid for.

SAM: Whaaaat? What damages?

CLARISSE: Mr. D'Baquel. Do you remember the house rules?

SAM: Yeah. So which one did I break?

CLARISSE: Most of them, sir.

SAM: Aw, this is unbelievable. Listen, this is a major scam if I ever saw one. You better believe that I'm reporting you guys to the Better Business Bureau when I get home!

JAKE: Sam?

SAM: What.

JAKE: I'd be happy to pay that for you.

SAM: I don't need you to pay it for me, thank you very little. Sam D'Baquel pays his own way, even if I think it's a crock that there were any real damages. *(To* CLARISSE.*)* You guys take Visa?

CLARISSE: No.

SAM: American Express?

CLARISSE: No.

SAM *(pulling out checkbook):* Fine. *(Begins writing check)* Gotta be back in the Stone Age, if the only thing you take is a personal—

(He stops cold, looking closely at his bill for the first time. He gapes at the bill, then CLARISSE, *then* JAKE.*)*

SAM: That's a little steep, don't you think?

CLARISSE: That's the price Innkeeper Fred set. A long time ago.

SAM: Well . . . I mean, can't we barter a little bit or something?

CLARISSE: Hold on. Let me check the policy guide.

(CLARISSE *plops a Bible on the counter, leafs through it, and thumbs to a particular place.*)

CLARISSE: Mmmm. Nope. No bartering. Sorry. (*Closes the book*)

SAM (*turning serious now*): I . . . I can't pay that.

CLARISSE: That's the price that must be paid.

SAM (*getting frantic*): Look, I'm really sorry I broke the rules. Can't you give me a break?

CLARISSE: Mr. D'Baquel, I'm sorry. This is the price that must be paid.

SAM: Well, that's just great! I can't pay that! You know I can't pay it! What am I supposed to do?

(*In saying this, he backs right into* JAKE. *He turns and regards his adversary with new eyes.*)

SAM (*to* JAKE): I can't pay it.

JAKE: I know.

SAM: I can't!

JAKE: Would you like me to pay it for you?

SAM: You . . . (*holding up bill*) I mean, do you see what it is?

JAKE: I know the cost. I'm still willing to pay it.

SAM: You'd do that?

JAKE: It's why my dad sent me here. That, and to help you with your baggage.

(JAKE *takes the bill from* SAM'S *hand and takes a long, slow walk to the door. He stops along the way and considers the sky, and his Father. For the first time in the play,* CLARISSE *is not dancing or smiling, but watching him somberly.*

    JAKE *opens the door, slowly climbs up on the railing overlooking the canyon, then turns back to face the room. He raises both hands in a crucifix position, and holds them there while pain begins to cross his face. Then he falls straight backward into the canyon.*

Sam runs to the railing in astonishment and looks down. What he sees makes him recoil at first. Then he takes a slower, more contemplative look.)

SAM *(to* CLARISSE*)*: Did you see that? Did you see what he just did?

CLARISSE *(checking her book):* Mr. D'Baquel, it appears your account is cleared.

SAM: My—?

(SAM *walks slowly downstage, thinking about what has just happened, his mood puzzled and reflective. He lifts one piece of luggage up on the table, begins taking items out of it and loading them onto the bellhop cart, one by one. It could just be bricks or small boxes with labels on them: Past Hurts, Envy, Revenge, First Marriage, Humiliation, Mistakes, Wasted Years . . . and a big one that says Sin.*

As SAM *continues unloading,* JAKE *reappears at the door, blood on his hands as though pierced by nails. He watches* SAM *with affection.* SAM *appears too weak to continue.* JAKE *arrives, puts a hand on shoulder, and begins helping him unload his burdens.*

Tentatively at first, then with increasing confidence, SAM *begins handing his burdens to* JAKE, *who places them on the cart. Fade down lights.*

HOST *emerges, speaks to the audience about the imagery of the play, and offers an invitation to receive Jesus right there. Following the response, the* HOST *exits.)*

SCENE 3

(Lights up on SAM *and* JAKE *again.)*

JAKE: Is that all of your baggage, Sam?

SAM: Oh . . . I'm sure there's a lot more that I've got to deal with, around here somewhere. But that's a pretty good start. Thank you.

JAKE: You're welcome. Now, one thing you need to understand about your new life, Sam. Everything isn't gravy.

Sam: Aw, it never was anyway. That just looked good on a T-shirt. It was all a charade.

Jake: And now?

Sam: Now?

Jake: Now that you've unloaded all of that . . . how does it feel?

Sam: How does it feel? How does it feel?

Jake: Sam?

Sam: How does it feel? *(He lets out a series of shrieks, like* Leonard. *Then . . .)* O'magoodness! O'magoodness, o'magoodness!

(He grabs Jake *by the arm, mimicking* Sabrina.*)*

Sam: Whoa.

(Lights down and Curtain)

Appendix

MUSIC NOTES

BAGGAGE CLAIM was first produced as *INNKEEPER FRED* at Capstone Theatre Company in Sacramento, Calif., in October 2004. Music selections, both in the body of the show and during scene changes, were integral to finding the script's full impact. Capstone used a small troupe of dancers to bring dance/human video elements to the in-script numbers. Some of the musical selections used:

SCENE	TYPE	SELECTION	NOTES
Act I Opener	Dance / Human video	*Revolutionary Love*, David Crowder Band	Energetic dance opener that featured the crazy guests arriving at the B&B
End of Act I, Scene 1	Scene changer-	*Help!* The Beatles	
Act I, Scene 2	Dance / human video	*Is It Any Wonder?* Nichole Nordeman	Other guests take a reflective look at the frozen D'Baquel family
End Act I	Dance / Human Video	*There Is No One Like You*, David Crowder Band	Energetic piece amps up the crazy guests and gives SAM a forum for frustration
Act II Opener	Dance / Human video	*Bring Me to Life*, Evanescence	Chilling backdrop for BRITTANY'S suicide moment, with demons op-

61

			pressing and Jesus delivering; most impactful moment of the show for many
End of Act II Opening	Scene changer	*I Wanna Hold Your Hand*, The Beatles	Perfect reversal to the Evanescence piece; brings us back to the happy pretend land
Act II, Scene 1	Background	*Coming Toward*, David Crowder Band	Instrumental background to IRENE and EDDIE'S soliloquies
Act II, Scene 1	Scene changer	*She Loves You*, The Beatles	Again, stark reversal of tone
Act II, Scene 1	Background	*Deliver Me*, David Crowder Band	The past of the guests is revealed . . . and so is the JAKE's true identity
End of Act II, Scene 1	Dance/ Human Video	*Here With Me*, MercyMe	Stirring song brings JAKE fully into his light as he reaches out to family members
Act II, Scene 2	Background	*I Remember You*, City on a Hill	Accompanies JAKE's ascent to the balcony and his fall into the canyon
Act II, Scene 2	Human Video	*Come Home Runnin'*, Chris Tomlin	Accompanies SAM'S unloading of his luggage . . . and JAKE helping him

PERFORMANCE LICENSING AGREEMENT

Lillenas Publishing Company
Performance Licensing
P.O. Box 419527, Kansas City, MO 64141

Name _____

Organization _____

Address _____

City _____ State _____ Zip _____

Play title: **Baggage Claim** by Don Bosley

Number of performances intended _____

Approximate dates _____

Amount remitted $_____

Mail form to Lillenas at the address above.

This is a royalty play. Permission to perform this work is granted when the Production Pack is purchased and the royalty is paid two weeks prior to the performance. Order your Production Pack for this script from your local bookstore or directly from the publisher at 1-800-877-0700.

ROYALTY: $35.00 for the first performance; $25.00 for each subsequent performance(s). Payable U.S. funds.

This play is protected by copyright. No changes or deletions can legally be made to the script without written permission from the copyright administrator. Please contact Lillenas Drama for more information on copyright laws.

Please feel free to photocopy this form.

GL # 450-100-390